FLOW OF THE HEARTBEAT

Q. J. WALKER

ISBN (paperback): 9781736152706

ISBN (e-book): 9781736152713

LCCN: 2020922770

Credits:

Cover Design: LeVance Alexander

Images: Under license from www.shutterstock.com

Saverson Flow Publishing

flowtempo840@gmail.com

CONTENTS

"KEY OF LOVE"

"RUNAWAY"

"JUST LET IT GO"

"LOVER'S ROMANCE"

"SOUL GEMS"

"MUSICIAN'S SOUL"

"NICE ONES"

"DUI"

"UNKNOWN"

"BUTTER"

"THINGS LEFT UNSAID..."

"TRAVELING"

"LUCKY I SUPPOSE"

"FOREVER LOVE"

"POWER"

"CORRECTIONS"

"JUST A LITTLE SPACE"

"IN THE WIND"

"CAN WE TALK?"

"CAN WE MATCH?"

"ELEVATE"

"THANKSGIVING"

"CHRISTMAS RAIN"

"GAZE"

"PATIENCE"

"VALUE"

"COMING HOME"

Love to all who have encouraged me through this journey.

FOREWORD

Robert Frost said it best, "Poetry is when an emotion has found its thought and the thought has found words." I have always been fascinated with poetry because when you read it, you get to see the soul of a person through their work. Poetry expresses emotion and the words flow straight from the heart. Q. J. Walker has written a book of poetry that captures moments in her life that the world has never seen. It captures the very essence of her soul and showcases all of her raw emotion put into it. In *Flow of the Heartbeat*, you get to see how Q. J. took her emotions during the highs and lows of her life, and streamlined them into thoughts she eventually wrote down to create her first soul filled poetry book.

Q. J. is a smart and loving person. More importantly, she is a talented poet who creates poems that will not only inspire you, but touch your soul. I hope the collection of written words in this book inspires each reader as much as it has inspired me.

Trina Davidson Brooks

Introduction

As I pour my soul out 2 you...

All I can do is pray you'll listen...

Not just hear words spoken but let them touch you within...

As I open up and let down these walls...

The flood of emotions race through and

I feel the calm come over me...

I'm at peace... the truth is set free...

"Eternal"

It flows through my body like blood in my veins...

It heals my soul when in pain...

It takes me far away when in joy...

Makes me wish for things longed for...

It's deeper than a pad and pen...

It's in my spirit, my soul... poetry...

"Unconditional"

As I write this you know words don't equal what you

mean to me...

my love for you is unmeasured...

I treasure every moment that we share...

a piece of my heart,

no you are my heart... I cherish it and handle it

with gentle care... even as time passes... the years

fade away... and we head to the afterlife u will

still be part of my life... our spirits are one...

Unconditional love.

"My angel"

You have taken your place on high...

and even though it's been a few years...

it only seems like yesterday

laughing, talking, and making jokes

now you flying high above

one of the angels

one of my angels looking down

I know you smile at all the good things I have done

laugh at all my silly moments,

and protect me from my unseen dangers.

"Gotta pray"

Dear father, as I sit back and think of all the

games. The ones played on me and the ones that I

did the same. Hearts broken... time wasted... now I've

given it all up... I've filled up my cup

and I'm praying father, for better days.

I understand the rain and some pain that we must

endure, but what if I see is the truth I shall go

through so I gotta pray... gotta pray...

"Stressed"

Life's trials seem at times too much to bear...
So much burden...
So much stress...
Looks like it will never be repaired...
They say never give up because your breakthrough is on
the rise
But all you see at the moment is a slow and painful demise.

You want to pull the trigger
Pop a ton of pills
Let your soul fly away
Your earthly body peels
Never knowing the impact, you made or left
Once you went away.

Yeah we're blessed, but life makes us stress
Even when you try to give your best
You're still left feeling stress...
Easy to run away
Easy to let go
Easy to say goodbye
Forgetting to fight for more so instead...

You want to pull the trigger
Pop a ton of pills
Let your soul fly away
Your earthly body peels
Never knowing the impact you made or left
Once you went away
Once you went away

"Preventive Ache"

Was told not to give love the cold shoulder...

I try but get pushed over...

Maybe I'm too vague...

Sometimes too direct...

Try to be a little subtle to see where it's headed at...

Can be a little aggressive but don't want to push you away...

So I ponder which direction to take and give a cold

shoulder to prevent heartache...

"Imperfections"

Full of imperfections...

all I can do is try...

see more of my good and less of my shortcomings...

I'm human and I fall repeatedly...

savior I know you're looking down on me...

I know your looking down...

seem like the dream has died...

even when I tried I fell short...

cry tears of pain...

inner and outer rain...

always seems like over yonder are greener pastures...

like the struggles are less to none...

"Angel in disguise"

"You never know when you're entertaining an angel..."

Never know when I let an angel pass me by...

ignored them...

didn't give them a chance to say hi...

wasn't dressed in a shiny suit...

more of dirt and shabby clothes...

but my eyes were on the glammed-out ones...

who think they are the gods and goddess of the states...

and the unknown person that was passed up... an angel that I misplaced...

"Oh well"

I think back and I can say I didn't give my all… was

scared to give my all… so we drifted apart… I didn't

know how to love, just knew how to play in this
game…

Didn't want to lose, but lost over and over again…pain

eventually felt on both ends… Who gives up? Who let
go?

Why keep trying? When it tends to be a show… who's

afraid? Who wants more? Who sheds a tear for the
love they want most? Who cries at night wishing
someone loved them for them and not their Nike…
Who wants more than some ass? Who wants to hear
about things in your past? Who wants to know you?

"Free your soul"

Only time and GOD can heal what's inside...

the smile hides the pain...

at night shed a little rain...

 past holds a tie...

even when you are told to let it go and break free..

No one knows your individual struggles...

no one knows...

Only GOD can help you free your soul...

"Hollow"

You can't see the cuts and bruises, but they are there..

Invisible to the eye, visible to the soul…

tears have flowed…

hearts have bled…

trying to find a place to be whole… want to love…

want to give of yourself but repeatedly raped internally…

the small hole becomes bigger and eventually leaving a hollow hole that was once a heart…

"The gamble"

So I lied
How else would I have gotten you on my side?
We know it's all fair in love and war
Don't be mad
It's a game
But in the game one thing remains
You would be good for me
And me for you

So I lied
Is that going to cancel us?
Yea yea I hear the it's all about trust
But I'm trusting you now
To let's make this work
For us

So I lied
I wanted you on my team
I've been thinking and dreaming
Had to make this a reality
Pull strings
Saying things
I had to get you
I had to get you

If you don't play
You don't gain
Sometimes you lose

But the gamble remains
A chance to win it all
So I'm betting it all

So I lied
How else would I have gotten you on my side?
We know it's all fair in love and war
Don't be mad
It's a game
But in the game one thing remains
You would be good for me
And me for you

"You are remembered"

Life seems long until someone is gone... then it's too soon... remember back in grade school... and K-A-G interludes... spirit in the wind... as we think of you... headed back to the place where it all began... my friend..

"Secrets"

We say one thing but be wishing another...

They say the truth will set you free but instead

We run for cover... I know the truth lies within... the

tongue just save face... as we continue to live life

among a bed of lies... secrets.

"Key of love"

In the key of love...

Your melody melts my heart...

The chord progression change

From a dissonant sound 2 one

Of hope, joy, rebirth...

A promise of things 2 come

All the trials have lead to

The thing that most pray 4

"Runaway"

Sometimes I want to runaway
but I know that I must stay
haunted by so many yesterdays
wondering if GOD is listening when I pray
It seems that now all I can do I is wait
And keep the faith

Broken hearted...
Broken dreams...
Broken spirit...
Lies in between
It's easier to runaway...
Runaway...

Sometimes I want to runaway
But I know that I must stay
Too much life to live
So much love to give
Heaven only knows how much pain I feel

Brokenhearted...
Broken dreams...
Broken spirit...
Lies in between
It's easier to runaway...
Runaway...

"Just let it go"

I got to find myself

I got to be free myself from your hold

I don't want to live in misery anymore

It's going to hurt like hell not to have you near

But you were a hindrance to my career

It was good when we first got together

Thought we could be as one

Things happen

Changes come

Moved to fast

Crash and burn

Life's lessons…

Leave their mark…

Just got to let go

Let go…of u…

"Lover's Romance"

Not a random encounter, our paths were to cross...

Fate saw fit to make two stars align...

As it did in another lifetime...

Here we are again...

Lovers and friends time and time again...

So I cannot pretend that this was all by chance...

Locked eyes as in a trance...

Engaged in a lover's romance...

"Soul Gems"

From the past to the present...

Falling in love is still possible...

Only time will tell...

Let it naturally flow...

As we take our time discovering soul gems...

"Musician's soul"

It's been awhile...
The times passes by...
But that smile last...
In my brain...
Trips out of town...
Gigs calling my name...
Can't complain...
Cause music flows and it brings more joy than
pain...
Or better yet it outweighs the typical 9 to 5...
So, baby just know...
I'll always come back...
You are my forever more...

I'll always come back...
Musician's soul...
This road is what feeds me...
So I travel to give them a part of me...
No one but u will have the heart of me...
I'll be back soon...
Until then the show goes on...
Musician's soul

"Nice ones"

It's a trip
How we have slipped
Fell off of what was once known as love
To chasing and fighting
To cursing and fussing
Seems like that's all you love
They say the nice ones finish last
and it seems to be true
Cause when I'm nice
That's when we are through
As long as I'm a dog
You tend to be a tick
Can't get you off my back
Where's the love in that?

"DUI"

As I look out the window...
As I look over my life...
I think of all the times I did u and u wrong...
How it was easy to hit and be gone...
How I left broken strings to die...
Broken... broken... broken pieces...
Pieces of your soul die when I left your side...
A string that I cut and I ran and I hide...
Because it's easier to walk away than to face you
And see tears roll down your face...
So dying souls... and broken, broken pieces...
As I look back and think of you and you and you...
Pain I inflicted and think of the root of my beginning
When I said forever with whom?
 Plucked my harp and said last movement last song...
So vowed to hit and run... and not get caught up
As now I'm DUI driving under infatuation...

Broken... broken... broken pieces...
Pieces of your soul die when I left your side...
A string that I cut and I ran and I hide...
Because it's easier to walk away than to face you
And see tears roll down your face...
Not get caught up
DUI driving under infatuation...

"Unknown"

Black and white mix...
Gray is formed...
Hues are in various shades...
Darker tone of gray leaving a lasting impression...
Lighter tones...
Subtle trace...
Never knowing when it ends and begins and but
Eventually it starts over again...
The shades of gray quite frankly cause...
Insanity...
Unknown on which route to take...
Insanity is what is claimed...
It's not clear cut and dry...
It's like fog as u walk through a maze...
Insanity is what is claimed....
It's unknown... too many shades...

"Butter"

Smooth as butter...

Things look so easy when you look down the street...

Come a little closer and I'll give you a dose of truth...

So many battles I had to endure...

So many nights I wanted to take my life just because it seemed too much to bear...

Only through many prayers and angels shielding me was I able to proceed...

It looks like its smooth as butter no dark days...

I made it through only by God's grace...

It is not over...

It remains...

"Things left unsaid..."

Looking at the hourglass...
Time has passed...
Sand continues to fall...
He looks at his phone...

Maybe if he had said things back then...
Would he be wondering?
Pushing u away only to truly wanting you to stay...
Crazy, crazy place...
A game of minds mixed with bottle of wine...
Only now to watch out for land mines...
With the things left unsaid...

Drowning into a bed of quicksand...
Grab the hand of this drunken man
Emotional state of regret...

Crazy, crazy place...
A game of minds mixed with bottle of wine...
Only now to watch out for land mines...
With the things left unsaid...

"Traveling"

Life lessons... life lessons...

I apologize if I release

I don't want to forever hold it in...

I want to be free...

Maybe what I say can help you, you, & you...

Maybe you can help me...

Steady traveling...

"Lucky I suppose"

you were my heart
for a moment in time
sometimes i think back
and press rewind

yeah...
I think back and press rewind
your heart wasn't mine to have
your heart isn't for the taken
locked away in a plexiglass
the key belong to another
lucky I suppose

guess one will never know
the only truth is
once upon a time
you held mine..

"Forever Love"

This time of year...
Want to give you a gift...
No present... no buying out the mall
Just give you love...
The thing that more than dollars combine

The thing that's not on the gram...
The thing that has holding power...
When the money gets low or fade
The love will remain...

Christmas and holiday time...
But it's an all-day thing...
A forever thang
Love, love, love...

So even as the years go by
You know how I feel...
Even when we disagree
The root of it all is love...
Forever love...

"POWER"

So this time around...
I said what I said
You got mad
Why can't we agree to disagree?
It's not meant to push you away
Only want to bring you closer...

The games that's played
Hard to say what we feel...
Don't want to lose control...
But still want something real...
It's hard to deal
We both want the power

We both want the power
We both want to win...
But we losing when we steady
Playing tug of war...
No one wanting to give up the control...
So we pull for power...

"Corrections"

Lines full of corrections...
Stop being hard on yourself...
Just a string of lessons....
Leading me to the one that gets me...
The one that I get...

Egos bruised...
Egos repaired...
Rejection to acceptance...
Chain of reactions...
Lines of corrections...

Send it out in the atmosphere
Let the universe
Send it here...
The journey it takes...
Not a straight shoot...
But a worthy race...
Once it's all said and done...
Lines of corrections...

"Just a little space"

yeah I know
I go ghost sometimes
yeah I know
just taking some time to clear my mind

I'm still thinking of you...
I still want you...
don't think I don't
just taking time to clear my mind

space not replacing your face
space to make you miss me when i'm away
I see you in my dreams...
I feel your energy...

on my mind...
you are still on my mind...
don't think i don't want you
just taking time to clear my mind

might seem like i'm ignoring you
just know it's still you
always you
forever you...

"In the wind"

Throw caution to the wind
Let's give in
No more waiting to be alone
No more waiting for the phone

Stop trying to pretend
Fighting the desire
That peeks out every time you speak
Call because I'm the one you seek

Time is moving
Let's not waste it
Years from now wishing we made it

"Can we talk?"

Heard a word today
Talked about forgiveness and turning the page
Let go of the hurt
Got to let go
Who knows who I've hurt along the way

Heard a word today
Talked about forgiveness and turning the page
I forgive me
I forgive you
Lord knows we all go through

Don't want to cause any harm
Life has given me enough scars...

Let's just turn the page...
Enough of the anger and pain
Love you through the fire...
Love you through the rain...

It seems to be simple but complicated at heart
If we laid down our guards and realize we all dealing with the same
Common theme... unresolved pain...

It seems to be simple but complicated at heart
If we laid down our guards and realize we all dealing with the same
Common theme... unresolved pain...

I love you for you...
I love you despite what you go through...
Can't judge because I'm broken too...

Broken creatures...
Healing cycles...
Soothing moments...

"Can we match?"

I'm a little crazy
But hey we all are
Can you're crazy match mine
Can you deal with my ways?
A rollercoaster of ways and moods
Demons and angels fighting through
Can you deal?

"Elevate"

Yeah, again, and again...
The journey I take...
Not a piece of cake
But sunshine on the other side...

Let the comments slide...
Let the haters hate
Let that be the gasoline
When you elevate...

When they pushed you to the side
Will see you again...
Then they try to pretend...
But one never forgets...
Just elevate...
As one pass-through

"Thanksgiving"

Thanksgiving blessings
Thanksgiving lessons...
From turkey to ham...
Greens to Mac n cheese

Thankful for all the blessings
From January to now...

Thanksgiving blessings...
Thanksgiving lessons...
It goes beyond a day in November
It's everyday as we inhale and exhale...
And be able to move around...
Thankful that we are still on solid ground

"Christmas Rain"

Last year it was all so sweet
Now you're gone and I feel uncomplete
Don't know why we fell apart
No reason...
On my end...
Try to call don't want to be only a friend...

You broke away so unexpected...
I tried and tried for awhile...
They said "let him go if it's meant he'll come back"

Now this holiday season
I won't have you around...
This holiday season
Will different from last few years
But I know next year will be better

With or without you...
I know it'll be ok
This Christmas I'll miss you
Next Christmas I'll be with someone new...

My heart will go on
My heart will link with the one who fits the mold
Continuing to love and live
Will be in our song...

This holiday season
My heart will go on
My heart will link with the one who fits the mold
Continuing to love and live
Will be in our song...

"Gaze"

Let's take a walk
Take a stroll
Chop it up
Look up at the sky
Gaze at the stars...
Dream and propel your mind to see more

Just chill
Just relax
Close your eyes
Dream...
Propel your mind to see more

The world is full of chaos...
Yet full of beauty...
Even though we knocking on 2020
Things are not different than the 60s...
Just different years same issues...

Let's take a walk
Take a stroll
Chop it up
Look up at the sky
Gaze at the stars...
Dream and propel your mind to see more

"Patience"

Seems like me doing right
Leads me to getting slapped in the face
Lord you know I'm trying
I'm trying
My patience is getting tested...

Seems like all the ones who do bad
Always winning
Lord I'm trusting in you
Feeling so down...
Feel like I'm in a storm...
Trying to find my way out...
Find my way to something better than the past
Find my way to what you have specifically had for me

Desire to love someone
Be faithful and true
Feeling like it's all a fantasy
Lord I know you hear me
Lord I know you see me
Lord I'm trusting in you

Lord I know you hear me
I need you
Forever and forever
I know you see me
Lord I'm trusting in you

"VALUE"

My value is too strong…
No need to keep hanging on…
My love is deep…
Only the right one can reach…
My value is too strong…
No time to waste…
Keep marching on…
Loving me
Keep loving me

Self-love
Self-care
Beautiful and worthy
God's child
Don't dim your light
Always shine regardless
Value is too strong
Keep loving yourself…
Keep loving yourself…

"COMING HOME"

The connection I was always seeking was right
there all along...
Going in circles...
Chasing things that were wrong...
 Instead of chasing after you...
After realizing that the ultimate connection will
always be with you... No one but you...
GOD patiently waiting for me to return home to
form the ultimate connection...
Patiently waiting...
Angels covering...
For the day I return home...
Now I'm home...
Forgive me for my wrongs...
I'm home... returning home to you GOD

About the Author:

Q. J. Walker, a native of Mississippi. Each of the poems in this book convey my thoughts, experiences, and observations. I write poetry to express my innermost feelings, unrealized dreams, missed relationships, moments in time. I also write to connect with people worldwide in a real and palpable way. As I express myself with these poems, my hope is that it deeply impacts the reader in a way that they can relate, even if only a little to these poems within their lives and thus create a connection.

Made in the USA
Las Vegas, NV
26 March 2021

20239467R00033